CATTINESS
SOME CATS ARE JERKS

CATTINESS
SOME CATS ARE JERKS

BY MARGARET CIOFFI

BLUE RIVER PRESS

Published by Blue River Press
Indianapolis, Indiana
www.brpressbooks.com

Distributed by Cardinal Publishers Group
A Tom Doherty Company, Inc.
www.cardinalpub.com

ISBN: 978-1-68157-071-6

Design: Margaret Cioffi
Editor: Dani McCormick
Photographs: Shutterstock

To Michael, the love of my life.
To Jodi, Todd and all my wonderful friends who
think I'm funny.

WE ALL LOVE CATS. Well maybe not all of us, probably about half the population, or a bit less, like maybe a quarter of the population loves cats, maybe not quite that many, but a bunch of people love cats. There's something about cats that folks who love them find very catty and cute, cute, cute. No two cats are alike. Besides being adorably cute, every cat has it's own catishes that are either delightful or obnoxious, or a combination of

 both. Most cats are a combination of lovey dovey and catanic all rolled into one adorable furry dickens. Sometimes they are absolutely wonderful and loving, and then other times they appear to be possessed by some sort of catevil. Kittens, however cuddly and adorable, are just as prone to cat moods as grown-ups. One minute they are curled up in a fluffy ball on your lap, and the next minute they are racing past you like you never existed, heading for a place to claw, a tissue to tear, or something to knock off a table. They will do this without so much as a sideways glance at you, the purveyor of those loving pats and scratches and yummy food. Nope, cats do not say thank you, never ever. You, loving human, have served your purpose, done your duty and they, the kittens or cats, have places to go, food to eat, naps to take, and your personal property to destroy.

9

*"If your cat falls out of a tree,
go indoors to laugh."*
Patricia Hitchcock

CATTINESS

There is a certain way cats look at and approach the world they live in. It is their world, not yours. You are merely a visitor. Cats rarely do what you expect or want them to do. It is always their call what they do and when they do it. Take meal time as an example. Kitty has praised (purring loudly is cat praise) your choice of food for weeks. Relishing every morsel with gusto. You, silly human, are tickled that you have finally found food that satisfies your feline friend. Then one day, out of the blue, Kitty no longer wants or likes your dinner offering. Quite the opposite. Kitty approaches the bowl, sniffs, sits down, sniffs again, turns to find you, and gives you a "I will not eat this slop" type of loud meow. The cat then flounces away to a corner and awaits a meal replacement you will undoubtedly rustle together as quickly as your pathetic human hands can. It's not fussiness, it's Cattiness. Cattiness is a certain something that cats have and do. Cattiness is the rule they live by. They never let anyone think they can be trained, controlled, or predictable, never ever. They are right to believe that; cats have a standard they live by and that is all there is to it. We humans are tolerated, and for some reason we don't mind all that much.

CATCHALL

Size doesn't matter one little bit when Kitty decides to take a load off. It could be anywhere from a tea cup to a wheelbarrow. If the **CATCHALL** is in use at the time Kitty decides to put her feet up, too bad, so sad. You, or whatever is taking up space in her soon-to-be resting place, will have no choice but to vacate. FYI–Never move a cat when the cat has made themselves comfortable. Not a good idea; no, sirree.

CATERWAULING

A meow is standard cat speak. At least, that's what we humans think. The real language of cats is **CATERWAULING**.

CATERWAULING can be heard when you wake your cat up before he is ready. When you have the nerve to give her a pat when a pat wasn't asked for. When you are late with dinner. Shame on you for trying to starve your poor adorable feline.

CATERWAULING can also be heard when you need to be reminded to clean the litter box. Whenever any of these misdemeanors occur you will be subject to verbal take down by Kitty.

13

CATPACK

A **CATPACK** is a feline SQUAD.

Cats are solitary critters. Generally, they do not like to share space or spend time with other cats. However, when they do come together, it's pretty powerful: strength in numbers and all that sort of thing. When travelling, a catpack usually speaks and acts as one if confronted by unwelcome attention of any sort. Beware of catpacks. You, oh friendly human, do not approach a catpack unless you are armed with fist full of cat treats that they, the pack, find satisfactory.

A CATPACK IS A FELINE SQUAD. Cats live in squads, no doubt about it. A Catpack is not an adorable collection of random kitties; a Catpack is a dangerous underground movement whose membership is limited to felines. Members of a Catpack are watching your every human movement. Be very careful. **CATPACKS** are dangerous.

14

CATDIARY

DAY 1 of my captivity–I am spirited away from my squad and three squares, no begging. I am thrust into a box and am transported to a place inhabited by small and large humans. I am plucked from the box without my permission and then handed around to various humans like a bowl of popcorn.

DAY 33–They have named Princess. I am not a Princess, I am a Queen. I cannot write. I am too angry.

DAY 46–My captors dine lavishly on fresh meat, while I am forced to eat tastless dry cereal. The only thing that keeps me going is the hope of escape, and the mild satisfaction I get from ruining the occasional piece of furniture. I'm partial to the work I did on an armchair.

CATALOGED

It's well known fact that cats dislike water. They will never thank you for giving them a bath. Wiping them off with a damp cloth will get you a hiss or two and perhaps a paw swipe (claws out). They are fully able to clean themselves, thank you very much, so any attempt to tidy them or freshen them up using water in any form will not be appreciated. If, through some sort of freak accident or human error in judgement, a cat finds himself wet or in water, he is waterlogged or **CATALOGED.**

INSTRUCTIONS: (HA GOOD LUCK!)

1. Completely bind cat in a towel

2. Apply pressure to cat's cheeks forcing his mouth open

3. Quickly, pop pill in cat's open mouth

4. Retrieve spit up pill from floor and try again

5. Repeat number three but hold cat's mouth closed for a count of twenty

6. Retrieve now-soggy pill and replace with fresh pill

7. Insert fresh pill into wide mouth straw

8. Repeat number two

9. Put the straw in your mouth and blow pill into cat's open mouth

10. Check online to see if the pill, which has been blown back and you have swallowed, is toxic or deadly to humans

11. Drink copious amounts of water to get the pilly, catty taste out of your mouth

12. Call your family doctor and make an immediate appointment

Dogs come when they're called. Cats, on the other hand, prefer you leave a message and they'll get back to you later. Perhaps.

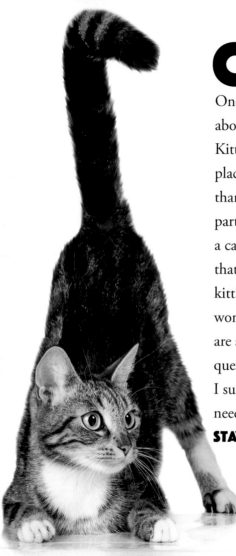

CATTAILS

One-minute, Kitty is sitting quietly, musing about all things cat, and the next minute, Kitty is attacking her own tail. The attack takes place with such vengeance and fury that you thank goodness it isn't one of your own body parts that is the recipient of Kitty's fit. Step on a cat's tail and you will get an instant reminder that the step was felt and painful, although kitties often exaggerate the pain. So you wonder how does Kitty not know that they are attacking their own tail? It's an excellent question, and one I cannot answer.

I suspect it has to do with boredom or the need to practice attacking. **CATS LIKE TO STAY IN TIP-TOP FIGHTING FORM.**

CATZILLA

Most days, that delightful little critter you adore is just that—delightful. You, oh silly human, believe that it is Kitty's nature to be delightful all the time. How could Kitty be anything but delightful? My, my, you are naïve. It's all a game, an act with Kitty. Kitty can and will turn into **CATZILLA** in one second for no reason whatsoever. Kitty is basking in the sunlight purring softly. Your perfectly even horizontal blinds let in enough sunlight for Kitty to luxuriate in. **OR DO THEY?**

YOUR KITTY IS A MARVEL OF ACROBATIC PROWESS. Kitty can fly through the air effortlessly, swing from one location to the next as if equipped with wings, and perch and walk in the tightest or narrowest of spaces. **KITTY IS A REAL CATROBAT.** If Kitty fails to land successfully, falls from her perch, or simply missteps, do not acknowledge the error or in anyway find it amusing. Kitty would not like that one bit.

CATROBAT

24

25

CATHOUSE

You pay your rent or mortgage
every month; it's your house.
Or is it? Kitty pays for nothing,
nor does Kitty offer any help with
the housework and repairs. Kitty
thinks everything is done magically.
Kitty isn't the least bit interested
in taking any sort of responsibility
for the maintenance, cost, or
upkeep of the accommodation lovingly
given. They are far too busy grooming,
basking, meowing, and sleeping. You should
know this.

IT'S NOT YOUR HOUSE, IT'S A CATHOUSE.

CABIT #1

THE LITTERBOX

A good thing about a cat is they pretty much clean up after themselves unlike house pets that bark. When Kitty is angry with you, and it doesn't take much to get on Kitty's bad side, Kitty will leave the poo in the litter box uncovered.

It is Kitty's way of letting you know who is boss. Never give Kitty the feeling that you are the dominant one in the relationship. If you persist in that type of behavior, you will soon realize that uncovered poo is just the beginning of Kitty payback.

When Kitty goes potty outside of the litter box, they are teaching we humans a lesson. If your Kitty has found a new location for a poo or two, you need to get to the bottom of Kitty's anger or the next poo locale will be in your favorite pair of shoes or nestled in the folds of your newest cocktail dress.

CATSPIRACY

You have planned a romantic evening with your partner. Dinner, wine, music, and a great movie on TV. You are all dressed up and ready for the evening. Kitty sees that you have gone the extra mile with dinner and is not happy. Spending time worrying about perfectly mashed potatoes, crisp salad, and glazed carrots has taken way too much time. You have neglected Kitty shamefully, and you will pay. Perhaps not right away, but things will happen. Unfortunate things.

BEWARE OF THE CATSPIRACY.

28

CATNAP

Cats sleep about seventeen to twenty hours a day. It isn't clear whether a good long nap makes Kitty more agreeable. Probably not. We humans tip toe past our sleeping feline careful not to disturb their sleep. Do we care that much that Kitty has uninterrupted sleep? Probably not. We are more frightened than caring. We know that if Kitty is awakened before the planned time it can be nothing but trouble for us humans. In future when Kitty is sleeping do not walk past Kitty, do not turn on music, ditto for the TV. Do not allow the phone to ring within earshot of Kitty.

YOU WILL LIVE TO REGRET DISTURBING KITTY'S CATNAP.

CATDIARY

DAY 95—Today my attempt to kill my captors by weaving around their feet while they were walking almost succeeded. I will try again.

DAY 141—I have mastered the art of puking on demand and have so far left deposits on their sofa, bed, and the mat in the front hall.

DAY 175—Slept all day so that I could annoy my captors with pleas for food and attention at ungodly hours of the night.

DAY 211—Decapitated a mouse and brought them the headless body, in attempt to make them aware of what I am capable of, and to try to strike fear into their hearts. One very loud scream later and I realize I was victorious.

DAY 237—I am convinced the other captive is a flunky. The dog is routinely released and, instead of running away, seems more than happy to return. He is obviously a half-wit who wags his tail incessantly, and that tongue, don't get me started on the tongue.

Why did the judge dismiss the entire jury made up of cats? Because each of them was guilty of **PURRJURY**.

CATGENDA

A Catgenda is a feline agenda. Cats like to stay organized and in control. If you think for one moment that you have control over your life, think again. Your cat was in the driver's seat the minute you brought him home. Meal times are not determined by you. The decision as to when dinner is served is entirely Kitty's. When to snuggle on the sofa, Kitty's call. How long you get to sleep; Kitty determines your sleep time. How long you are allowed to read the newspaper; again not your decision. It is a known fact that a cat will do exactly as it pleases at all times. You, servant of Kitty, can try all you want to make Kitty do something other than what is on his catgenda, but you will fail. Cats are their own master. You are their servant and must honor their **CATGENDA**. It is wise to remember this.

CATURDAY

You look forward to the weekend: two days of doing whatever you want. Your plans include sleeping in, and taking your time drinking your coffee and reading the paper, and maybe a nice long soak in the tub followed by a stroll around your garden. All these things would be possible if it weren't for your adorable kitty. Kitty has waited patiently all week for Caturday. Yes, Caturday. It is wise if you remember it is Kitty's day, not yours. It's the day he gets to snuggle in bed with his paw across your mouth. Your newspaper reading is the ideal time for Kitty to catch up on pawlotics. A relaxing soak? Forget it. Lolling in a tub will not be tolerated by Kitty. It matters not that the bathroom door is closed. Remember

CATURDAY is Kitty's day, not your day.

CATANKEROUS

You've just fed your fish. You stand and watch them swim around the tank surfacing occasionally for food. You love your fish and because you love it, you have filled the fish bowl with what you are sure your fish will like. Ferns, buildings, rocks, and pebbles: an underwater world. Kitty is watching quietly off in the corner. She is waiting for the moment when you tire of watching your fish swim around endlessly. The time comes when you leave your spot in front of the fish bowl and then exit the room. Kitty leaves her spot in the corner and positions herself beside the fishbowl. Victory is close at hand. Score one for Kitty, AKA **CATANKEROUS.**

What do cats like to eat for breakfast? Mice Krispies.

CABIT #2

MEOW

Kitty has a meow for almost every occasion. It is up to you to figure out what each meow means. Kittens meow to communicate with their moms. Grown cats meow for us humans. There is the "I'm hungry" meow that, when ignored for a long period of time can end up with a "Kitty in your face screeching" meow. The "I'm bored" kind of meow that is usually followed by an out of the blue act of aggression.

The "I'm sick or hurt" meow is a kind of pitiful, sad sound that can be a real heart tugger. One thing humans should steer clear of is mimicking a meow. Even if you think you are good at cat meows, do not practice within Kitty's earshot. Kitty hates that and will punish you in ways you haven't even thought of.

36

A cat isn't fussy, just so long as you remember he likes his milk in the shallow, rose-patterned saucer, and his fish on the blue plate. From which he will take it, and eat it off the floor.

Arthur Bridges

38

CATCALL

Rare is the kitty who has but one sound. Cats emit several different sounds depending on their mood. There is the casual meow, kind of like a hey-how-are-ya. The hated early morning meow is one most cat lovers have experienced. It begins as friendly good morning purr that turns into a get-out-of-bed-and-feed-me scream if ignored.

The get-out-of-my-way-I'm-on-a-mission meow is fairly loud, crisp, with a bit of a warning included. The loud, rather intimidating do-it-again-and-you're-toast meow is uttered to put you in your place. The stop-turn-hiss-and-screech is not really a meow, but more of a battle cry. It is emitted when Kitty is cornered, or you step on its tail, you clumsy beast.

Finally, there is the all-out loud and angry verbal Kitty assault or **CATCALL** that can be brought on by anything from being served chicken rather than salmon to being picked up and moved to an unsatisfactory spot away from the sun.

CATARRANGED

Your guests are set to arrive in an hour. You've cleaned your home thoroughly. Fresh towels in the bathroom, pillows plumped and placed on the sofa, and your newest coffee table books arranged attractively. You've filled several vases with flowers and several bowls with candy. Your wine is chilling; glasses are sparkling and ready to be used. Your cat is standing by his bowl waiting for it to be filled. You stand back and admire the fruits of your labor, ignoring Kitty completely. You have just enough time to get changed and be ready to greet your guests. You head to your bedroom with a smile on your face. Kitty also has a smile. As you carefully choose your outfit, retouch your makeup, and arrange your hair, Kitty is busy rearranging your pillows and books, moving your vases of flowers to the floor where they belong, dumb human, and making sure the sparkling glasses you have set out are **CATARRANGED** by size. Small broken glasses in front, then the medium broken and large broken at the back. **FYI, IT'S NEVER A GOOD IDEA TO IGNORE KITTY.**

Why is the cat so grouchy? Because he's in a bad mewd.

41

CATARACT

Cats are actors–**CATARACTORS**. They play act at loving your company. They pretend they enjoy your gentle pats and cuddles. You think they love how you pick them up, without their permission. They let on that the stupid feather on a wire or the dumb wind up mouse that you wave at them is all in fun and enjoyable. Kitty is acting, putting on a **CATARACT**.

While you are busy dreaming up even more ways to have fun with Kitty, Kitty is working on her own idea of fun. Once Kitty sets the stage, it will soon become apparent what Kitty really thinks of your idea of fun.

CATSUIT

If you thought the word Catsuit meant a one-piece outfit worn primarily by women, you would be correct, unless of course you are Kitty. As far as Kitty is concerned, a catsuit is whatever suits him. If it suits him to sit on your lap and be gently petted, then you will be allowed. However, if it suits Kitty to leap out of a doorway, drawer, or from behind a curtain and attack with claws out, that is also a catsuit. Basically, a catsuit is whatever Kitty feels like doing or suits how he feels at any time of the day or night. **WHATEVER SUITS KITTY IS A CATSUIT.**

43

CATERNITY

Your cat is about to become a mom and you are over the moon. You have so many friends who have expressed a desire to have one of her kittens. Of course, they don't know Kitty the way you do. Oh, you pretend that she is the most loving and adorable cat in the world. A cat incapable of mean or nasty behavior. But you know that your thoughts are wild, wishful thinking. The reality is Kitty is one ornery cat. She has her moments of nice, but they are usually a way of getting her way. With kittens on the way, you're already not-so-nice cat has turned into a real catzilla. **CATERNITY** doesn't suit her, and she is none too happy with her current situation, and she is certainly not happy with you. She looks at you like it was your fault she is pregnant. There doesn't appear to be any brand of food in the universe she likes. Even the delicious homemade meals you prepare for her are sniffed at. With multiple kitties on the way, you wonder if they will be as demanding and obnoxious as their mom. After much consideration, you decide to find other accommodation for yourself until such time as you have managed to find homes for her offspring.

45

CATALIST

Kitty is staring off into space. You aren't sure what Kitty finds so fascinating but you are sure it is a special cat thing that we humans couldn't possibly understand. Several minutes go by and Kitty is still off in her own world. You begin to worry. Could Kitty be plotting some sort of cat payback for the shortage of her favorite dinner? Could Kitty be holding a grudge because the litter box wasn't the level of pristine Kitty expects? What could it be that has rendered Kitty so still and quiet. Now you are frantic. Perhaps getting Kitty's attention with a favorite cat treat will snap her out of it. Maybe some catnip. As you contemplate your next move you look up as Kitty lists ever so slightly to the left. Kitty is asleep, perched on an angle—a **CATALIST.**

CABIT #3

HISSTERICAL

Whenever Kitty hisses, you should really consider it a warning shot. Many cats when afraid or agitated will let you know that it is time to back off with a hiss. The hissing is a pretty shocking thing if you aren't used to being disciplined by Kitty. It's a good time to give Kitty space and time to regroup and settle down. Often Kitty will have a hissy fit when a stranger or strangers are in the house. In order to avoid hissiness particularly in front of guests, put Kitty's favorite food and creature comforts in another room. Kitty will happily leave you and your guests alone when presented with that kind of attention. Sometimes Kitty hisses because she simply feels like being obnoxious. The same advice applies, leave her alone to hiss her heart out.

CATALEPSY

You realize that Kitty has been incredibly quiet for the last several minutes. You stare at Kitty, unsure why she has suddenly become completely still. Is she having a health crisis? You don't know what to do. Should you: A. pick up Kitty and hug the dickens out of her; B. call her by name in the hopes of snapping her out of whatever her problem is; C. get some food you know Kitty loves, perhaps a treat of some sort, or; D. leave Kitty alone? 'D' is the recommended course of action. Do not disturb Kitty whilst she is in a state of **CATALEPSY**. Kitty isn't sick, hungry, or in need of a cuddle. Kitty is planning her next assault. If you interfere, you could be the assault victim.

CATANIC

You are having one of those lovely cozy moments, just you and Kitty. Kitty's soft purr lulls you into a wonderful relaxing mood. You are one with your cat. There is nothing at all wrong in the world, nothing until you decide to rearrange your seating position ever so slightly. Fool. You have disturbed Kitty, and because you have disturbed Kitty, you will pay. That cuddly fluffy little bundle of joy has become an ornery, prickly beast that no longer purrs but hisses. Claws that were in are now out, and you and the chair you are seated on will pay for the disruption. Your cat has become the devil.

Positively **CATANIC.**

CATFETERIA

Unlike humans who enjoy company whilst eating, cats prefer solitude when eating. No sharing of the food dish, and absolutely no tasting or testing by other members of the family, pets or otherwise. If Kitty's dinner is touched or tainted in any way, be prepared to replace said dinner immediately.
Kitty does not like group or **CATFETERIA** type dining one little bit.

CATISH

Every cat has at least one catish. A catish is similar to a fetish, only catty. How a Kitty develops a catish is anyone's guess. They probably develop a catish because they can. To a cat, a catish is a part of their life, and they enjoy them. To we humans, they are often downright annoying. You can't cure Kitty of his catishes, nor can you train him to stop. Training a cat to do anything is like teaching a squirrel to salsa dance. A catish can be anything from preferring his food in a small white saucer-like bowl to preferring whole milk to 2%. A **CATISH** can also be Kitty's preference for a pillow covered with a100% Egyptian cotton pillow case with a 400 thread count.

CATHLETIC

We all know that cats are pretty fit. They are **CATHLETIC**. You would think that sleeping more than seventeen hours a day would render them flabby and lackadaisical. For some reason, even the most rotund of cats has a certain cathleticism. Kitty is always keen to show or demonstrate her athletic prowess to humans. Leaping onto a ledge, the back of a chair, or a bookcase are just some of the basic demos Kitty is happy to present. For a truly Olympian demonstration of Kitty's cathleticism, sneak up on Kitty as she is playing with the mouse-like toy or scrunched up piece of paper you recently purchased. You will see a demonstration of four-legged and two-legged dancing, prancing, swiping, kicking, and leaping that is worthy of Olympic gold.

"*Cats will amusingly tolerate humans only until someone comes up with a tin opener that can be operated with a paw.*"
Terry Pratchett

CATASTROPHE

Your favorite mug, the green one with the big handle is sitting empty on the counter. You meant to put it away but got busy. Kitty has always liked the green mug. Probably because you like it, and because you like it, Kitty wants it. You have left the room and your favorite mug unattended and unprotected. Kitty gets up from her comfy spot and strolls over and then jumps up on the counter for a closer look at the mug. She looks around, not that she cares if someone is watching, it is more that she is curious to see if you will come back to guard you property. Too late though, your favorite mug is now Kitty's. She sniffs it, caresses it and then for whatever cat type reason deftly bats the hell out of it, a **CATASTROPHE.**

"*The problem with cats is that they get the same exact look whether they see a moth or an ax-murderer.*"
Paula Poundstone

CATAPULT

Sailing through the air with effortless grace, the cat proves its physical as well as intellectual superiority. Finding the secret of personal flight requires brainpower we humans do not possess. There isn't a reason in particular that the cat cannot take to the ground like most other non-flying beings wanting to effect a change in location. But then cats aren't like every other being in the universe they prefer to **CATAPULT.**

CATEGORY

Sometimes Kitty likes to say thank you for the cat treats, the good food and the clean litter box.

The manner of thank you varies from allowing you to watch as she heaves up a rather large fur ball or, if feeling particularly grateful, to presenting you with the bottom (or top) half of their latest bird or rodent kill. Sharing is something Kitty does on occasion and it should be appreciated. Accept Kitty's offering with grace and gratitude. Do not look repulsed or recoil when the offering is presented. It may appear to be gory but remember it is **CATEGORY** direct from Kitty's heart.

CATATONIC

"*I had been told that the training procedure with cats was difficult. It's not. Mine had me trained in two days.*"
Bill Dana

You are sitting quietly in your comfy chair, enjoying the music playing in the background. You have just opened your book. It's the newest book by your favorite author. There is a cup of tea on a little table by your chair ready for you to enjoy. All is peaceful and quite wonderful. You have worked hard all week and this is your reward. An hour or so of complete relaxation surrounded by the creature comforts you love. You look around wondering where Kitty is. You love Kitty, but this is your special time and Kitty is often demanding. Before returning to your book you take one last look around and then you spot Kitty off in the shadows of the room staring at you. Kitty is angry. She is scheming, mentally calculating how she can get even with you for forgetting to include her in your plans. You go back to your book hoping to forget the look you saw in Kitty's eyes. Never take your eyes off Kitty. In a second Kitty is on the back of your chair cuddling and purring. Perhaps including Kitty in your reward time is a good thing. Just as you settle in and continue your reading Kitty uncurls, rises up on her hind legs, and swings at your cup of tea knocking it to the floor. Tea is spilled on your new book making chapter one illegible. Your clothes are soaked, as is the chair. Kitty has left the scene. You scramble to stop the tea ruining the recently refinished little table. Kitty was angry with you and has gotten revenge. Kitty is curled up by the window, getting even is the perfect tonic–

CATATONIC.

CATERPILLAR

You thought the purchase of a scratch post or pillar would stop Kitty from destroying your furniture. You jokingly refer to the scratch post as a **CATERPILLAR**. You had put a lot of thought into the purchase. You didn't settle on the first one you saw. You considered the happiness of Kitty. When you presented the 'caterpillar' to Kitty, she seemed pleased and knew exactly what it was for. You smiled as you looked fondly at your newly upholstered sofa and chair. You leave for work happy in the knowledge they are safe from Kitty destruction. Or are they?

You have carefully chosen the brand and type of cat food for your precious kitty. You are sure, as a result of your loving attention to cat food detail, you will be able to spend a loving evening in the company of your fluffy friend. You carefully clean and wash Kitty's favorite food bowl. Once dry, you are ready to fill said dish with a flavor of food from one of the excellent selection you have spent so long choosing. You, oh loving human, because you made a special trip to the pet store to purchase the excellent selection, are excited to see the thrill in Kitty's eyes when you present the carefully chosen meal.

You fill the dish with a mound of food and present it to Kitty. You stand smiling down at Kitty. You are waiting for the thank you meow that follows when you have presented a satisfactory meal. It doesn't come. No meow, no nothing, just a paw swat at the dish, a this-food-is-crap hiss, and a walk away. You really must learn to do a better job of **CATERING** to Kitty.

PURRS AND PAWS

Cats have a way of communicating that is unique and, at times, annoying. We tolerate Kitty's various communication styles because we simply adore everything about our feline friend. They, on the other hand, tolerate us. Oh, they have their moments when they will show us some sort of affection with a gentle lick, a warm purr, or gentle stroke of their paw. These affectionate demonstrations are dependent entirely on whether you have delivered the things Kitty wants. The perfect meal, a clean litterbox, several suitable resting places, and a good petting whenever Kitty wants one.

PURRSONALITY

Every cat has a different way of looking at life and you. Some cats are very tolerant and will give you a couple of chances to get dinner right. Others are less tolerant and will let you know instantly that they are not pleased with your dinner performance. A common cat retaliation is a paw swipe followed by a hiss. Your Kitty could decide to mete out a harsher punishment – like the loss of your favorite chair for an entire evening, the destruction of an article of clothing you were particularly fond of, or the heaving up of a fur ball just as you are about to dig into your evening snack. Cats has dozens of ways to demonstrate their unique **PURRSONALITY.**

PURRCHASE

Cats love to chase their tails. One wonders if they actually know it's their tail or think it's some other cat's tail. They will actually try and make the attack on their tail a surprise. Kitty will employ a purrchase approach. They purr softly as if nothing is amiss and then, when they are sure the phantom owner of the tail isn't looking, they will attack, chasing their tail around and around.

A perfectly executed **PURRCHASE.**

PAWLYWOOD

You hardly ever see cats in movies. Dogs will perform in front of a camera for dog treats. Cats would never perform for less than ten percent of the gross profit.

PAWLITICS

Cats aren't the least bit pawlitical. They could care less who is running the show as long as it is understood that they are in control.

PURR COAT

Cats love to have their purr coat stroked and combed. Nothing brings out Kitty's good side than a gentle pet and stroke. Once the process of petting Kitty has begun, it is wise to remember that it isn't up to you when to stop. Kitty will let you know when you are finished. When you are allowed to stop, Kitty will purr loudly, stretch, stand, flick her tail, and sashay out of the room. Once her fur coat is a purr coat Kitty heads for a soft comfy spot to catch a few relaxing moments of sleep.

CABIT # 4

HUGGING AND SNUGGLING

Just because we believe hugging is a sign of affection and the more hugs we give and get the better, it doesn't ring true with cats. If you're a hugger and snuggler, curb your enthusiasm. Kitty will not thank you for your overt affections. A gentle hug is permitted, but enough with the squeezy, huggy stuff. Oh, never pick up Kitty while she is sleeping or eating. It is so not done. Of course, if you are totally fearless and don't mind sparring with an unhappy cat, have at it. Kissing is another thing, cats are frankly baffled by kissing. Kitty likes to show affection with a full on butt in your face display. Perhaps humans should consider butt displays as a show of affection instead of hugs. Just a suggestion.

CATHEDRAL

Most people think of a Cathedral as a place of worship. Kitty's idea of a Cathedral is pretty similar except that it is a place of worship to Kitty. The location for this worship is anywhere of Kitty's choosing. It could be your favorite chair, atop your Great Aunt Laura's antique hall cabinet, or it could be right in the midst of the most delicate, hand-made, imported lace table cloth you recently purchased. Worshipping Kitty in her chosen locale is simple. Bring gifts of food, whimsical toys, and bowls of rich cream. Lay them down in front of Kitty and then leave. Kitty prefers privacy in her **CATHEDRAL.**

CATITTUDE

Kitty walks into a room, slowly taking in the inhabitants, the furniture, and whether there is a decent spot to put down for a while. You, oh human, can do nothing but wait. Kitty is not in a hurry and may not even stay in the room. What to do? Do you pat the spot beside you, "C'mon Kitty, come sit with daddy," or do you ignore Kitty? Your answer comes quickly. Kitty leaps onto the sofa and takes the spot where your book is currently sitting. Kitty glares at you, does a few quick claws at the book to let you and the book know who is boss, then sits down. It is important to remember that Kitty has a finely honed **CATTITUDE** that you, oh snivelling human, cannot and should not ignore.

DOGS AND CATS AND DIFFERENCES

1. Dogs, being an interested and engaged pet, will attempt to under stand what you are saying by tilting their heads. Cats will meow loudly to drown out your conversation then saunter away and take a nap.

2. Dogs are trained to walk on a leash. Cats will not tolerate a leash or training of any kind.

3. Dogs come when called. Cats will ignore any request for their presence. It's a power thing with cats.

4. When you come home from work, a dog will be always be happy and excited to see you. Cats will still be mad at you for leaving in the first place.

5. Dogs will give you unconditional love until the day they die. Cats will make you pay for every mistake you've ever made since the day you were born.

6. Dogs will wake you up if the house is on fire. Cats will quietly sneak out.

7. Dogs love to be hugged and petted. Cats tolerate your hand on them only if it comes with their favorite cat treat attached.

8. Dogs are always sorry for anything they have chewed and destroyed. Cats are proud of their destruction and happily present their handiwork to you.

9. Dogs will try their best to sit quietly by your side as you watch TV. Cats will sit on the TV.

10. Dogs will eat off the floor. Cats prefer dinner to be served on a gold trimmed Royal Doulton dish.

CATTACHMENT

Kitty rarely develops a **CATTACHMENT** to anything. However, every so often, for some weird catty reason, Kitty takes a shine to an object. It could be a stuffed toy you purchased for Kitty or it could be your absolutely most favorite of all times silk scarf. Whatever the object, once Kitty has developed a cattachment, it is no longer retrievable, nor does it belong to anyone but Kitty. Kitty will lick it, knead it, roll all over it, and hug the heck out of it.

Kitty will carry it around, tuck it in her cat bed, or simply keep the item in her eyeline. Don't even think about touching or removing the object; the Kitty consequences are not worth thinking about.

Q: What is a cat's favorite color?
A: Purrrple!

86

CATTY

Every cat believes they have style. This cattitude is obvious when watching a cat sashay past you. They would never say it but they are absolutely convinced they are superior in every way. They believe their aloofness, fussiness, and catitude give them their catty style.

A cat maintains her catty style with several good washes daily. You will never see a Kitty wearing anything but clean sleek fur and a simple and attractive collar or a tasteful hat in a color that is complimentary. If you spot a cat wearing or looking less than catty do not under any circumstance say anything to upset or offend Kitty.

Cats are not natty–they're **CATTY.**

"The way to get on with a cat is to treat it as an equal–or even better, as the superior it knows itself to be."
Elizabeth Peters

CATWALK

You are having an average Caturday. You have done the things you needed to do, shopping, cleaning, and cooking, and decide it is time for a break. You make yourself a cup of tea and sit down to relax for a few minutes. Kitty seems to be occupied and so you have no fear of interruption. Just as you are relaxing you notice Kitty walking along the hall. Your eyes follow behind her. You find yourself studying her gait. After a few seconds you realize your cat isn't walking, your cat is strutting. Your cat has a swagger, and a rear wiggle that is almost sexual. Kitty has a sashay, a sassy hop, a silky stroll; it's called the **CATWALK.**

"Cats never listen. They're dependable that way; when Rome burned, the emperor's cats still expected to be fed on time."
Seanan McGuire

CATFIGHT

Cats don't fight the way dogs do. They have to be provoked and will fight when no other option is available to them. Cats consider themselves lovers not fighters. You will never see a cat embroiled in a battle with another cat without a good reason. Kitty would rather lounge around, clean herself or sleep than take part in any sort of altercation. Kitty gets more mileage with her hisses than her claws. A **CATFIGHT** usually begins with a hissing contest and, if unresolved, turns into a cat brawl that you should steer clear of. It can get pretty ugly.

90

CATERAN

Cats are the hit and run type of warrior. They will never initiate a fight. Starting a fight is so not their style. They will jump into the fray, if they feel like it, make a couple of hisses, again if they feel like it, take a few swats with a paw, maybe bare their teeth, and then they will head for the hills. It's called **CATERAN**.

CABIT # 5

KITTY GIFT GIVING

Cats show they care by gift giving. Their gifts are usually a dead rodent, bird, or butterfly. As far as Kitty is concerned, these are tremendously generous gifts. Of course you, oh squeamish human, have a different opinion. You should know that demonstrating care, or dare I say love, is not something Kitty normally does. Presenting their human with some dead critter is the highest form of cat love you will ever experience. It is selfless and Kitty doesn't even require a reward for her goodness. Seeing you smiling and happy is all the reward Kitty requires.

92

CATABOLIC

Most cats could care less about toys. They will tolerate a wind-up mouse or a catnip filled toy, but only just. They will play with them for a limited period of time, and mostly to please us humans. However, Kitty does enjoy playing with a ball. She likes the chase a ball gives her. Racing after it, catching it, flipping it into the air, swatting at it and chasing it again. It is a challenge, and a game that Kitty loves. Once Kitty has worn herself out she will often take the round object to a favorite quiet spot. She will nestle the object between two paws, hunker down, and bite then **CATABOLIC** the heck out of it.

SNAPPY NOT HAPPY

SIGNS KITTY IS NOT HAPPY!

Kitty can change from happy to snappy in less than a second. It is important for you to recognize the signs indicating Kitty is less than cheery. It is imperative that you give Kitty space when he is unhappy. If you want to stay on Kitty's good side, you will respect his mood and steer clear. It's not a good idea to get in Kitty's way when he is snappy not happy.

BACK-OFF

If you ever hear Kitty growling or making guttural moans, step way back and give Kitty her space. She is about to have a massive feline melt down and you do not want to be around when it happens. Kitty is telling you to back off, best you take Kitty's advice.

TAIL ACTION

Unlike dogs, when cats swish their tails it isn't a sign they are happy to see you. Tail flicking is a sign Kitty is cheesed off. The faster Kitty's tail moves, the angrier she is becoming. The hair may also stand up on an angry cat's tail. Leave the room immediately and let Kitty get it out of her system.

SHIFTY EYES

Kitty's eyes may dilate to adjust to the light in the room, but they can also be a sign that she is totally angry. Often we humans get mislead and ignore the evil eye Kitty is sending. It is easy to make that mistake. The best way to avoid Kitty's wrath when the dilation of her eyes has to do with anger, not sunlight is to completely avoid any contact with Kitty.

95

BODY MOVES

If Kitty arches her back and her fur stands on end it means she is totally cheesed off. Her fury is percolating at record speed, so it is best to let her get it out of her system.

SWATTING

Think of cat swatting as a warm up to the big event—a cat brawl. Swatting can sometimes be taken for playfulness on be the part of Kitty. It is, on occasion, meant to be playful. It is always best, however, to take it as a warning shot. Do not try and play with Kitty when she starts swatting. She is in combat mode, not play mode.

BIG TROUBLE

The minute your cat crouches down in striking position or pins back her ears, you need to leave the room. Kitty is about to let it fly and you do not want to be anywhere near Kitty when that happens.

CATACOMB

We humans are never sure how Kitty will feel about being catcombed.
They generally prefer to do all their own personal care. When approaching
Kitty with grooming in mind, it is always a good idea to keep your
grooming tools out of sight. You may be ready to give Kitty your idea of a
spa treatment, but it doesn't follow that Kitty is. Best to approach the
process slowly. Sit with Kitty on your lap. Gently pat her until she is
relaxed. Whilst doing this, quietly say flattering words like 'Pretty Kitty',
'You are a beautiful Kitty, yes you are', and so on. Continue with the
patting and words of love until Kitty is almost comatose. Once she is in a
state of total relaxation, bring out your grooming tools. Very gently begin
catacombing Kitty. It would be very foolhardy to try anything that Kitty
would consider aggressive or annoying.

CATATOMIC

Similar to catatonic but way more dangerous to humans. Kitty is staring at you as if in a catatonic state. You're sure it is just a cat thing and Kitty is merely relaxing her brain with mindless thoughts of nothing in particular. You would be wrong. Kitty is **CATATOMIC**, plotting her revenge in case you do something now or in the future that will upset Kitty. Catatomic happenings can be anything from a massive hiss, to a double claw scratch, or a quick and hefty paw swipe directed at your favorite figurine.

CATFALLS

Catfalls are different, very different, than pratfalls. A pratfall is a joke. Something someone does to entertain. A catfall is no joke. You should never look at a catfall as a joke, something Kitty did to entertain you. Kitty would never catfall to entertain you. Don't even think of laughing or even chuckling if you witness a catfall. Kitty considers herself very agile, and graceful. The way she walks, climbs, even the way she sleeps is elegant. When Kitty sometimes, not often mind you, but sometimes misses a step and **CATFALLS** you must pretend that you didn't notice. It's better that way.

CATTERY

Cats are vain. Why else would they spend hours grooming themselves and indulging in hours and hours of beauty sleep. Yes, the fluffy little wonder that you adore is actually extremely narcissistic. Kitty loves cattery, feline flattery, in every form. Whether you brush and pat her coat for hours, tell her how pretty she is, or simply stare lovingly into her beautiful eyes, it is all the same to Kitty. It is **CATTERY** pure and simple, and Kitty deserves all the cattery she gets. She is, after all, the most wonderful creature on the planet.

CATCHUP

Most cats will avoid playing games with you unless it pleases them. They need to be in the mood and will play only by their own rules. As an example, if you toss a small foam ball at Kitty, she may retrieve it. Operative word is 'may'. If she decides to retrieve it, she will bat it around a little and then whack it back in your direction. You, silly human, dying to make Kitty your playmate, will immediately toss the ball back. Once the ball has returned to Kitty she will look at it, pick it up and walk away with it firmly lodged in her teeth. Game, set, and **CATCHUP.**

CATSCAN

Cats have a way of looking at you that can be off putting. A catscan is a squinting of the eyes that begins with a slight almost unnoticeable narrowing of the eye and continues until Kitty's eyes appear to be almost closed. The **CATSCAN** can feel like they are seeing right through you. When you get one of his nasty stares, you often wonder what you have done to deserve it.

You should wonder. The catscan is a shot over the bow, a precursor to some sort of punishment you will get. Your punishment could come in the form of a hairball artfully arranged in your slipper, or perhaps a refusal to eat the meal you have lovingly served Kitty. A **CATSCAN** is an early warning sign and should be taken seriously.

> *"A dog will flatter you, but you have to flatter a cat."*
> *George Mikes*

Q: Why did the cat cross the road? A: It was the chicken's day off!

CATGILITY

Cats seemed to be able to balance themselves on the narrowest of ledges and make it look as if they had an eight lane highway to walk along. They can jump from one location to the next with rarely a mishap or misstep. It is their catgility that allows them to sneak up on you wherever you are. You could be relaxing, eyes closed, in a tub full of bubbles and warmth. When you open your eyes, you nearly leap out of the tub–there, perched on your back scrubber, is Kitty. Sometimes Kitty will stroll along the top edge or your headboard and watch you sleep. If Kitty does happen to lose her balance and fall, she will always land on her feet. It's her **CATGILITY,** plain and simple.

CATIVITY

Even though cats sleep away seventy-five percent of their day, they still manage to be pretty cative. Their cativity takes many forms: bursting into a run for no particular reason, whacking the heck out of their scratch pole or your Louis the 14th armoire, or slapping a relaxing Fido until he howls. Kitty's burst of cativity is impossible to explain or understand. Once Kitty has burned off her excess energy, her cativity usually reverts to sleeping, cleaning, kneading, sleeping, eating, and then sleeping again.

CATVENTURE

Whenever Kitty manages to sneak out of the house, he doesn't hang around. No sir. Kitty likes to engage in a **CATVENTURE** or two. Heaven knows where he gets to, but he is definitely on a mission. You, loving human, become worried when Kitty is gone for over an hour. You needn't worry. Kitty will return when he is ready, not a second before. Kitty is busy checking out the neighborhood, seeing what other cats have, assessing what he wants, and making a mental list of demands. You, oh dumb human, are so happy to see Kitty stroll up the path to your house that you will give Kitty anything he wants.

CATSTRUCTION

Cats are not builders or architects. You will never see a cat reading *Architectural Digest*. They do care what their own home looks like, but it is a personal thing. The place they live must absolutely adhere to their rigorous cat standards. They need their private space, several lounging areas, a tidy dining spot, and a well-appointed toilet area. If any of these requirements are not met, then Kitty will do some **CATSTRUCTION** to bring things up to Kitty code.

109

CATTENTION

Cats have an excellent cattention span. They can sit still and watch you, the TV, or your family forever and never seem to waver or get distracted. They just sit and stare. Perhaps we are wrong and haven't captured Kitty's cattention at all. Maybe instead Kitty has hypnotized herself or she is asleep with her eyes open. Whatever Kitty is doing whilst staring, never get comfortable with it. Kitty can change in a second.
One moment she is mesmerized, so it seems to you anyway, by whatever you are doing, and the next minute she is on the attack. There is no way you can ever expect to capture and keep Kitty's **CATTENTION** unless she lets you. That will never happen.

CATTLE

Cats are not fighters. They would never start or pick a fight. They just don't care enough about anything or anybody to get riled up. A cattle is rare. Kitty would need to be pretty cheesed off to get into it. Hissing and gesturing are about the extent of Kitty's cattle strategies. If, however Kitty does decide to put up her dukes, look out. The claws come out, teeth are bared, and Kitty's fur is standing on end. Kitty is ready to do cattle. The expression "fur flying" is exactly what happens when the cattle ensues. Kitty is looking for submission from her foe, sort of like an admission of wrongdoing.

CATICURE

When Kitty needs a good scratch, she heads for her scratch pole. Giving her claws a workout on the pole is a bit like a manicure for Kitty. Kitty just loves it. She uses her time on the scratch pole to relax and do some serious thinking. It is important that there is a scratch pole for Kitty. If none is available, stupid human, then be prepared for Kitty to give herself a caticure on any of the furniture you have in your home.

Keeping her claws in good order is important to Kitty. She will meticulously clean her claws first before her caticure. After she is finished, Kitty will go off and find someplace to have a nap.

CATICURES totally relax Kitty, sort of like a meowsage for her claws.

Q: Why did the cat cross the road?
A: It was the chicken's day off!

112

"Cats can work out mathematically the exact place to sit that will cause most inconvenience."
Pam Brown

113

CATHODE

Cats are not story tellers. They like to keep everything to themselves. If they ever decide to tell a cathode, it would most likely be a complaint rather than an actual story. A cathode is a cat story with a twist. If Kitty is having a problem with other cats or pets in the neighborhood, she will often come to you with her complaint. You, humble servant of Kitty should be attentive and listen to her complaint, even if you can't understand her. Kitty doesn't expect you to do anything. She can easily handle any situation. Kitty simply want to be sure that you are on her side and sympathetic. Gesture knowingly, nod in the appropriate places, and offer Kitty her favorite cat treats as a way to show your appreciation for the way she shared her **CATHODE** with you.

114

CATAPHOR

A cataphor is like a cat metaphor. A touch of drama that Kitty
will employ when trying to get her point across. If Kitty has been
bothered by the attentions of the dog, she will use a dramatic
cataphor to let you know that he is behaving badly towards her.
Her method of communicating, obviously not verbal as you don't
speak cat, will be by physically demonstrating her plight. If the
dog is the problem, then Kitty will wait until she and the dog are
both in your company before she demonstrates via **CATAPHOR**
what her problem is. It could be sitting on the dogs head, clawing
at his butt, or simply meowing loudly in his face.

ADMIT IT, YOU'RE
A CAT PERSON

Recognizing you are a cat person isn't a bad thing really, although being referred to as a crazy cat lady isn't terribly flattering. You are someone who loves the aloof nature of a cat. The lack of dog-like adoration doesn't bother you. Nor does Kitty's moodiness and fickleness upset you. You are happy in the knowledge that if anything, heaven forbid, should happen to you, Kitty will find happiness in another home, no problem. Actually, you probably aren't happy at all knowing this. It is downright upsetting that after all the things you do for your cat, all the sacrifices you have made, and all the love you have given Kitty she can forget all about you in a second or less.

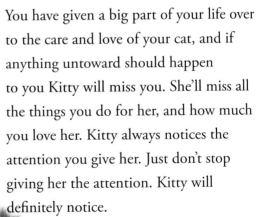

You have given a big part of your life over to the care and love of your cat, and if anything untoward should happen to you Kitty will miss you. She'll miss all the things you do for her, and how much you love her. Kitty always notices the attention you give her. Just don't stop giving her the attention. Kitty will definitely notice.

Your friends and family complain that they don't see or hear from you much anymore. You often lie to them about your absences. You tell them you are working a lot of overtime lately. Sometimes you tell them you've had a troubling flu or cold which you didn't want them to catch. The reality is you are home with Kitty watching TV and cuddling. Going away on business or for a weekend with friends is often nerve racking for you. You become anxious and wish that Kitty had a cell phone. Ridiculous right. You have cat person syndrome when your Kitty has a wardrobe bigger and better than yours. Even though cats hate being dressed in anything but their own fur you have spent oodles on little outfits for your cat. Meanwhile your own wardrobe is in serious need of an upgrade. When you have friends over and Kitty curls up to one of them in a familiar manner you actually become jealous. That's right, you get jealous.

MEOW

CATTY WORDS

Catabolic Licking and biting a ball

Catacomb Kitty hairdressing

Catalepsy A Kitty stare

Catalist Catnap on an angle

Cataloged Waterlogged Kitty

Catanic Satanic Kitty

Catankerous Kitty's own stocked fishbowl

Cataphor Cat metaphor

Catapult Cat leap

Cataract Cat acting

Catarranged Kitty room staging

Catastrophe Feline disaster

Catatomic Unpleasant Kitty behavior

Catatonic A cat trance-like state

Catcall Cat noise

Catchall A cat resting place

Catching Kitty fetching

Catchup Kitty soccer

Category Thank you gift from Kitty

Caternity Kitty is pregnant

Cateran Strike and run cat fighting

Catering Choosing Kitty's food

Caterpillar Scratch pole

Catering Choosing Kitty's food

Caterwauling Real language of cats

Catfeteria Cat dining area

Catgenda Cat agenda

Catgility Proof that cats are superior

Cathedral Worshipping Kitty

Cathletic Athletic Kitty

Cathode Cat story

Caticure A cat manicure

Catish Feline fetish

Cativity Kitty hobby

Catmosphere Perfect cat space

Catnip A warning bite

Catpack Feline squad

Catrene Kitty toilet

Catrobat Kitty acrobat

Catscan A warning look from Kitty

Catspiracy Feline conspiracy

Catsuit Whatever suits Kitty

Catstruction Kitty Construction Company

Cattention Zen Kitty

Cattery Cat flattery

Cattle A cat battle

Cattiness The rule cats live by

Cattitude Cat attitude

Catty Natty

Caturday The start of Kitty's weekend

Catventure It is never just a walk

Catzilla Feline Godzilla

ACKNOWLEDGEMENTS

I would like to thank the friends and family who laughed at everything I read them and encouraged me to keep on writing. I also want to thank my husband Michael who is convinced I am brilliant. What can I say, he loves me, and I him. Finally, I would like to thank every Kitty out there for being animals worth writing about.

ABOUT THE AUTHOR

Margaret Cioffi works as a creative director and consultant in the advertising business. She is the author of several books. She lives in Toronto, Ontario with her husband Michael.